Table of Contents

Chapter 1: The Evolving Terrain: Overview of the Current Restaurant Industry Landscape

Chapter 2: Starting and Planning a Restaurant: Crafting the Blueprint for Success

Chapter 3: Legal and Regulatory Considerations: Navigating the Legal Landscape of Restaurant Management

Chapter 4: Financial Management: Navigating the Fiscal Waters of Restaurant Operations

Chapter 5: Marketing and Branding: Crafting a Distinct Culinary Identity

Chapter 6: Menu Development: Crafting Culinary Excellence

Chapter 7: Staff Management: Nurturing a Positive and Productive Work Environment

Chapter 8: Overcoming Challenges in Delegation: A Manager's Guide Navigating Obstacles: Strategies for Effective Delegation

Chapter 9: The Pitfall of Ego in Restaurant Management: Breaking Down the Barriers Ego as a Barrier: A Hindrance to Effective Transactions

Chapter 10: The Manager's Role in Accountability: Orchestrating Excellence Leadership Accountability: Setting the Tone

Chapter 11: The Owner's Responsibility: Cultivating a Culture of Accountability Owner's Oversight: Aligning Vision and Accountability

Chapter 12: Direct Communication with Employees: Bridging Gaps in Ownership Insight

Chapter 13: Strategies for Managing Crises: Navigating Uncharted Waters Navigating the Storm: Crisis Management Strategies

Chapter 14: Nourishing Success: The Impact of Employee Meals on Restaurant Culture

Chapter 15: Unlocking Performance: The Strategic Role of Bonuses in Motivating Management Teams

Chapter 16: Ikigai, Embracing Purpose and Passion in Hospitality

In the vast and dynamic landscape of the modern restaurant industry, a myriad of influences is   the way culinary entrepreneurs approach management. As we embark on this exploration, it's crucial to dissect the current state of the restaurant landscape, identifying trends that have emerged as well as the challenges that restaurant owners and managers grapple with on a daily basis.

Chapter 1:The Evolving Terrain: Overview of the Current Restaurant Industry Landscape

The Culinary Tapestry: Culinary Diversity and Fusion

The culinary world is experiencing a renaissance, with diners seeking more than just a meal—they crave an experience that transcends traditional flavors. This shift in guest expectations has given rise to culinary diversity and fusion. Restaurants are no longer confined to serving cuisine rooted in tradition; instead, they are embracing innovation by blending various culinary influences. From Korean-Mexican fusion tacos to Thai-Italian amalgamations, the contemporary restaurant menu is a tapestry of global flavors that caters to the increasingly adventurous palate of the modern guest.

Green Gastronomy: Health and Sustainability

A growing awareness of health and environmental concerns has permeated the restaurant industry. Guests are not only mindful of what they eat but also how their food choices impact the planet. Restaurants are responding by prioritizing fresh, locally sourced ingredients and adopting sustainable practices. From farm-to-table initiatives to eco-friendly packaging, the emphasis on health and sustainability is not merely a trend but a fundamental shift in the ethos of modern dining establishments.

Bytes and Bites: Technology Integration

In an era dominated by technology, restaurants are leveraging digital innovations to enhance the guest experience and streamline operations. Online reservations, contactless payments, and mobile ordering have become commonplace, aligning with the expectations of a tech-savvy clientele. The integration of technology extends beyond guest-facing interactions, influencing backend processes such as inventory management and data analytics. Embracing these digital tools is not just a choice; it's a necessity for staying competitive and meeting the evolving demands of the modern guest.

Beyond the Table: Delivery and Takeout Dominance

The rise of food delivery platforms has disrupted the traditional dine-in model, offering guests the convenience of enjoying restaurant-quality meals in the comfort of their homes. Restaurants are increasingly joining forces with delivery services to expand their reach and tap into new markets. This shift has implications for menu design, packaging considerations, and the overall guest experience. Navigating the nuances of delivery and takeout is now a critical aspect of modern restaurant management.

Shifting Palates: Changing Guest Behavior

The landscape of guest behavior is undergoing profound changes, driven by social, cultural, and economic shifts. The desire for convenience, the impact of remote work, and global events like pandemics have all contributed to a transformation in how, when, and what people choose to eat. Understanding and adapting to these shifts is imperative for restaurants seeking to align their offerings with the preferences of today's discerning guests.

Navigating the Currents: Key Trends and Challenges

Crafting Experiences: Emphasis on Experience

Beyond the culinary journey, guests seek immersive and memorable experiences. Restaurants are investing in creating unique atmospheres, interactive elements, and personalized services to differentiate themselves in a crowded market. From themed interiors to chef's table experiences, the emphasis on creating moments that linger in the minds of patrons is a trend that underscores the evolving nature of the dining experience.

Data as the Compass: Data-Driven Decision-Making

In the age of information, data has emerged as a powerful tool for restaurant managers. Analyzing guest preferences, optimizing supply chain management, and making informed business decisions are now facilitated by the wealth of data available. Restaurants that harness the potential of data-driven insights gain a competitive edge, allowing them to adapt swiftly to changing trends and guest behaviors.

Virtual Culinary Realms: Rise of Ghost Kitchens

A paradigm shift in the restaurant industry is the emergence of ghost kitchens, also known as virtual or cloud kitchens. These establishments operate solely for fulfilling online orders, eliminating the need for a traditional brick-and-mortar space. This model offers a cost-effective way for restaurants to reach a broader audience and experiment with new concepts. The rise of ghost kitchens represents a seismic change in how culinary entrepreneurs approach the notion of physical dining spaces.

Chapter 2: Starting and Planning a Restaurant: Crafting the Blueprint for Success

In the dynamic and vibrant world of the restaurant industry, the journey of starting and planning a restaurant is a thrilling adventure, marked by creativity, strategic thinking, and meticulous planning. This chapter is a comprehensive guide that delves into the foundational elements of this journey, including concept development and market research, business plan essentials, and the critical considerations of location and layout. As we navigate through these key aspects, the central theme remains clear: the creation of an establishment where the guest experience is paramount.

Concept Development and Market Research: Unveiling Your Culinary Identity
Crafting Your Culinary Vision: Concept Development

At the heart of every successful restaurant is a compelling and unique concept that not only aligns with the passions of the creators but resonates with the desires of the intended guests. Concept development is the art of crystallizing this culinary vision into a tangible and appealing form. It involves defining the type of cuisine to be offered, shaping the atmosphere, and identifying the distinctive elements that will set the restaurant apart.

Imagine a canvas where culinary creativity meets guest expectations. Are you envisioning a sophisticated fine-dining experience, a cozy and casual eatery, or perhaps a trendy and vibrant cafe? The concept should not only reflect your culinary prowess but also consider the preferences and expectations of your intended guests. It's about creating an experience that transcends the mere act of dining and leaves a lasting impression.

Understanding Your Audience: Market Research

Market research serves as the compass guiding your restaurant concept toward success. A deep understanding of the target market is essential, involving the analysis of demographics, psychographics, and local trends in the area where the restaurant will be established. This phase is not just about understanding culinary preferences; it's about deciphering the pulse of the community, identifying gaps in the market, and assessing the competitive landscape.

Conducting surveys, interviews, and competitor analyses are crucial steps in gathering insights into the preferences and expectations of potential guests. What cuisines resonate with them? What dining experiences are they seeking? The knowledge gained from market research ensures that your concept aligns seamlessly with the desires of your target audience, setting the stage for a restaurant that not only meets expectations but exceeds them.

Business Plan Essentials: Building a Roadmap for Success
The Blueprint of Success: Crafting Your Business Plan

A comprehensive and well-crafted business plan is the foundational document that outlines the trajectory of your restaurant venture. It serves as a roadmap, guiding the restaurant from its inception to sustainable profitability. Each section of the business plan plays a crucial role in providing clarity to both the creators and potential investors.

- **Executive Summary:** This succinct overview encapsulates the essence of your restaurant concept, its mission, and key objectives. It's the appetizer that stimulates interest and sets the tone for the rest of the plan.
- **Company Description:** Here, you provide detailed information about your restaurant, including its legal structure, history, and the ethos that defines its identity.
- **Market Analysis:** A thorough examination of the target market, competition, and industry trends. This section demonstrates a keen understanding of the external forces that will impact your restaurant.
- **Organization and Management:** Details about the organizational structure of your restaurant, key team members, and their roles. Investors want to know that your team is well-equipped to navigate the challenges of the industry.

- **Service and Product Line:** A detailed description of your menu, service style, and any additional offerings such as catering or events. This section outlines what makes your culinary offerings unique and appealing.
- **Marketing and Sales Strategy:** An exploration of how you plan to promote and market your restaurant, along with the sales tactics that will drive revenue.
- **Funding Request:** If seeking financing, this section outlines your funding needs, how the funds will be utilized, and the expected return on investment. It's the financial narrative that convinces potential investors of the viability of your venture.
- **Financial Projections:** The financial heartbeat of your business plan, including income statements, balance sheets, and cash flow projections. This section demonstrates your understanding of the financial intricacies of running a restaurant and showcases the potential for profitability.
- **Appendix:** Supporting documents such as resumes of key team members, lease agreements, and any other relevant information that strengthens your case.

A meticulously prepared business plan is not only a tool for securing funding; it's a strategic document that aligns all facets of your restaurant business, providing a solid foundation for decision-making and growth.

Location and Layout Considerations: Positioning for Success
Choosing the Right Spot: Location Selection

The importance of location in the restaurant industry is akin to the selection of the perfect stage for a performance. The right location can elevate your restaurant to stardom, while a poor choice can pose substantial challenges. Location selection involves a thorough analysis of various factors that directly impact the restaurant's visibility, accessibility, and resonance with the target audience.

Consider the foot traffic in the area, the visibility of the location, and the presence of potential competitors. Is the location easily accessible by both pedestrians and vehicles? Does it align with the demographics and preferences of your target market? Proximity to key amenities, cultural hubs, or business districts can significantly influence the potential success of your restaurant.

Chapter 3: Legal and Regulatory Considerations: Navigating the Legal Landscape of Restaurant Management

As a restaurateur, navigating the legal and regulatory landscape is a critical aspect of ensuring the smooth and compliant operation of your establishment. In this chapter, we will delve into three key areas of legal consideration: licensing and permits, health and safety regulations, and employment laws. Understanding and adhering to these legal frameworks are essential for maintaining the integrity of your restaurant, safeguarding the well-being of both guests and staff, and avoiding potential legal pitfalls.

Licensing and Permits: Securing the Legal Foundation
The Regulatory Tapestry: Licensing and Permits

Licensing and permits form the legal foundation on which your restaurant operates. Obtaining the necessary licenses is not just a legal obligation; it's a prerequisite for opening your doors to the public. The specific licenses required may vary based on factors such as location, type of establishment, and the services you offer. Here are some common licenses and permits that restaurateurs often need to secure:

- **Business License:** This is a basic requirement for operating any business legally. It authorizes your restaurant to conduct business in a specific location.
- **Food Service License:** A crucial permit that authorizes the preparation and sale of food. Health departments typically issue this license after inspecting your kitchen and ensuring compliance with food safety standards.
- **Alcohol License:** If you plan to serve alcoholic beverages, you'll need an alcohol license. The type of license may vary, ranging from beer and wine licenses to full liquor licenses.
- **Building and Occupancy Permits:** These permits ensure that your restaurant complies with local building codes and occupancy regulations. They cover aspects such as fire safety, accessibility, and structural integrity.
- **Music and Entertainment License:** If your restaurant offers live music or entertainment, you may need a license to ensure compliance with copyright laws and local regulations.
- **Outdoor Seating Permit:** If you plan to have outdoor seating, you may need a permit to use public space for this purpose.

Navigating the licensing and permitting process can be complex, involving interactions with various government agencies. It's crucial to research and understand the specific requirements in your jurisdiction and initiate the application process well in advance of your planned opening date.

Health and Safety Regulations: Prioritizing Guest and Staff Well-being
A Commitment to Wellness: Health and Safety Regulations

Ensuring the health and safety of both guests and staff is a paramount responsibility for restaurant owners. Adhering to health and safety regulations not only protects individuals but also safeguards the reputation of your establishment. Here are key considerations in this domain:

- **Food Safety Standards:** Compliance with food safety regulations is non-negotiable. This involves proper food handling, storage, and preparation to prevent contamination and foodborne illnesses. Regular inspections by health departments help ensure ongoing compliance.
- **Sanitation and Hygiene Practices:** Maintaining a clean and hygienic environment is essential. This includes regular cleaning of kitchen equipment, utensils, dining areas, and restroom facilities. Establishing clear protocols for

staff hygiene, such as handwashing and the use of gloves, further contributes to a safe dining experience.
- **Allergen Management:** With the increasing prevalence of food allergies, managing allergens responsibly is crucial. Clearly labeling menu items, training staff on allergen awareness, and having processes in place to prevent cross-contamination are vital aspects of compliance.
- **Occupational Health and Safety:** Ensuring the safety of your staff involves compliance with occupational health and safety regulations. This includes providing a safe working environment, conducting regular safety training, and addressing potential hazards in the workplace.
- **Emergency Preparedness:** Having protocols in place for emergency situations, such as fires or medical emergencies, is essential. This includes training staff on evacuation procedures, maintaining emergency exits, and having first aid supplies readily available.
- **COVID-19 Protocols:** In the wake of global health crises, adherence to specific health protocols, such as social distancing, mask-wearing, and sanitation measures, has become crucial. Staying informed about evolving guidelines and adjusting your practices accordingly is imperative.

Regular staff training, documented procedures, and ongoing communication are key elements in ensuring that health and safety standards are not just met but consistently maintained.

Employment Laws: Navigating the Workforce Landscape
Balancing the Employment Equation: Employment Laws

The relationship between an employer and employees is governed by a complex set of employment laws. Complying with these laws is not just a legal obligation but also contributes to a positive work environment and the long-term success of your restaurant. Key areas of consideration include:

- **Minimum Wage Laws:** Familiarize yourself with local, state, and federal minimum wage laws to ensure that your employees are compensated appropriately. This includes understanding any variations for tipped employees.
- **Working Hours and Overtime:** Establish clear policies regarding working hours, breaks, and overtime. Compliance with regulations governing overtime pay is essential to avoid legal issues.
- **Equal Employment Opportunity (EEO) Laws:** Discrimination and harassment are serious issues in the workplace. Understanding and adhering to EEO laws ensures a fair and inclusive work environment.
- **Workplace Safety:** Beyond health and safety regulations, additional laws govern workplace safety. This includes providing a safe working environment,

training employees on safety protocols, and addressing any reported hazards promptly.
- **Employee Contracts and Agreements:** Clearly define the terms of employment through contracts and agreements. These documents should outline expectations, job responsibilities, compensation structures, and any non-disclosure or non-compete clauses.
- **Employee Benefits:** Understanding the requirements for providing employee benefits, such as health insurance and retirement plans, is crucial. Compliance with relevant laws ensures that your employees receive the benefits they are entitled to.
- **Employee Classification:** Properly classifying employees as either full-time, part-time, or contract workers is essential. Misclassification can lead to legal challenges and financial penalties.
- **Termination Procedures:** Establish clear procedures for terminating employment, including adherence to notice periods and compliance with relevant laws. Unlawful termination can result in legal consequences.

Chapter 4: Financial Management: Navigating the Fiscal Waters of Restaurant Operations

In the dynamic world of restaurant management, financial acumen is a cornerstone for success. This chapter delves into key aspects of financial management, covering budgeting and financial planning, cost control and pricing strategies, as well as the critical functions of accounting and bookkeeping. A robust financial strategy not only ensures the viability of your restaurant but also provides a solid foundation for growth and sustainability.

Budgeting and Financial Planning: Crafting a Financial Roadmap
The Art of Fiscal Navigation: Budgeting and Financial Planning

Creating a comprehensive budget and financial plan is akin to charting a course for your restaurant's success. It involves forecasting revenues, estimating expenses, and establishing financial goals. Here are essential elements to consider:

- **Sales Projections:** Begin by estimating your expected sales. Consider historical data, market trends, and the impact of any planned marketing initiatives. Sales projections serve as the foundation for the entire budgeting process.
- **Operating Expenses:** Identify and categorize your operating expenses, including rent, utilities, payroll, marketing, and supplies. Creating detailed line items helps in understanding where your money is allocated and facilitates effective cost control.

- **Capital Expenditures:** Factor in any significant capital expenditures, such as equipment purchases or renovations. While these may not be recurring, they impact your overall financial health and should be planned for strategically.
- **Cash Flow Management:** A cash flow statement is crucial for understanding the timing of cash inflows and outflows. This helps in identifying potential cash flow gaps and ensures that you have the necessary funds to cover operational needs.
- **Contingency Planning:** Anticipate unforeseen circumstances by incorporating contingency plans into your budget. This could include setting aside funds for equipment repairs, sudden market shifts, or other unexpected challenges.
- **Financial Goals:** Establish short-term and long-term financial goals. These could include achieving a certain level of profitability, expanding your restaurant, or paying off debt. Clearly defined goals provide direction and motivation.

Regularly reviewing and updating your budget allows you to adapt to changing circumstances and make informed financial decisions. It serves as a dynamic tool for financial management rather than a static document.

Cost Control and Pricing Strategies: Balancing Act for Profitability
Economic Stewardship: Cost Control and Pricing Strategies

Cost control is a critical aspect of restaurant management, directly impacting profitability. Effective cost control involves managing both variable and fixed costs. Here are key considerations:

- **Menu Engineering:** Analyze the profitability of each menu item by considering the cost of ingredients, preparation time, and popularity. This allows you to identify high-margin items and optimize your menu for profitability.
- **Supplier Negotiations:** Build strong relationships with suppliers and negotiate favorable terms. This includes exploring bulk purchasing discounts, securing competitive prices, and regularly reviewing supplier agreements.
- **Inventory Management:** Implement efficient inventory management practices to minimize waste and control costs. Regularly assess inventory levels, rotate stock to prevent spoilage, and optimize par levels based on demand.
- **Labor Cost Control:** Labor costs are a significant part of restaurant expenses. Monitor labor efficiency, schedule staff based on demand, and consider cross-training employees to enhance flexibility.
- **Pricing Strategies:** Establish pricing strategies that balance profitability with customer expectations. Consider factors such as competitor pricing,

perceived value, and market trends. Implementing dynamic pricing for special events or peak hours can also optimize revenue.
- **Technology Integration:** Leverage technology for cost control and efficiency. Implement point-of-sale (POS) systems that integrate with inventory management and provide real-time sales data. This allows for better decision-making and reduces the risk of errors.

A delicate balance between cost control and pricing strategies ensures that your restaurant remains competitive while maintaining healthy profit margins.

Accounting and Bookkeeping: Financial Records as the Compass
The Financial Compass: Accounting and Bookkeeping

Accurate and transparent financial records are the foundation of sound decision-making. Accounting and bookkeeping serve as the lens through which you gain insight into the financial health of your restaurant. Consider the following elements:

- **Accrual vs. Cash Accounting:** Decide whether to use accrual or cash accounting methods. Accrual accounting recognizes revenue and expenses when they are incurred, providing a more comprehensive view of financial performance. Cash accounting records transactions when cash is exchanged.
- **Chart of Accounts:** Develop a detailed chart of accounts that categorizes income and expenses. This provides a clear structure for recording transactions and generating financial statements.
- **Regular Financial Reporting:** Generate regular financial reports, including profit and loss statements, balance sheets, and cash flow statements. Analyze these reports to track performance, identify trends, and make informed decisions.
- **Reconciling Bank Statements:** Regularly reconcile your bank statements to ensure that your financial records accurately reflect your actual cash position. This helps in identifying discrepancies and mitigating the risk of errors.
- **Tax Compliance:** Stay informed about tax regulations and ensure compliance. Keep meticulous records of income, expenses, and deductions to facilitate the tax filing process. Consider consulting with a tax professional to optimize your tax strategy.
- **Internal Controls:** Implement internal controls to prevent fraud and errors. This includes segregating duties, conducting regular audits, and restricting access to financial systems.
- **Cloud Accounting Solutions:** Explore cloud-based accounting solutions that offer real-time access to financial data and streamline the bookkeeping process. These solutions enhance collaboration and provide scalability as your restaurant grows.

Maintaining accurate financial records is not just a legal requirement; it is a strategic imperative for informed decision-making and long-term financial health.

Chapter 5: Marketing and Branding: Crafting a Distinct Culinary Identity

In the bustling landscape of the restaurant industry, marketing and branding are essential components that not only attract guests but also establish a lasting connection with them. This chapter explores the art of building a strong brand presence, leveraging social media and digital marketing, and implementing customer loyalty programs. By mastering these elements, you'll not only entice new guests but also foster a community of loyal patrons who champion your culinary venture.

Building a Strong Brand Presence: The Culinary Identity
Crafting Your Culinary Identity: The Foundation of Branding

In the world of gastronomy, a strong brand presence is built upon a clear and compelling culinary identity. Your brand is not just a logo or a name; it's the sum total of the experiences, emotions, and perceptions that guests associate with your restaurant. Consider the following elements to craft a distinct culinary identity:

- **Define Your Unique Selling Proposition (USP):** Identify what sets your restaurant apart from the competition. This could be a signature dish, a unique culinary concept, or a specific ambiance. Your USP forms the foundation of your brand.
- **Create a Memorable Visual Identity:** Develop a visually appealing and memorable brand identity that includes a logo, color scheme, and design elements. Consistency in visual elements across your physical space, menus, and marketing materials reinforces brand recall.
- **Cultivate a Unique Atmosphere:** The ambiance of your restaurant contributes significantly to its identity. Whether it's a cozy and intimate setting, a trendy and vibrant space, or a sophisticated fine-dining experience, the atmosphere should align with your culinary vision.
- **Tell Your Story:** Share the story behind your restaurant. Highlight the inspiration, the journey, and the passion that went into creating your culinary venture. Storytelling humanizes your brand and resonates with guests on a deeper level.
- **Consistent Brand Messaging:** Ensure that your brand messaging is consistent across all touchpoints, from your website and social media to in-house signage and promotional materials. Consistency builds trust and reinforces brand authenticity.
- **Guest Engagement:** Actively engage with your guests to build a sense of community. Respond to reviews, encourage user-generated content, and create opportunities for guests to share their experiences. A strong brand is built through meaningful interactions.

By defining and consistently reinforcing your culinary identity, you establish a brand that goes beyond the plate, creating an emotional connection with your audience.

Social Media and Digital Marketing: Navigating the Digital Culinary Landscape

Digital Culinary Exploration: Social Media and Digital Marketing

In the digital age, a robust online presence is instrumental in reaching and engaging with your target audience. Social media and digital marketing strategies amplify your brand message and extend your culinary reach. Consider the following strategies:

- **Choose the Right Platforms:** Identify the social media platforms that align with your target demographic. Instagram, Facebook, Twitter, and TikTok are popular choices for restaurant marketing. Tailor your content to suit the platform and engage with your audience.
- **Visual Storytelling:** Leverage the power of visual storytelling through high-quality images and videos. Showcase your culinary creations, behind-the-scenes moments, and the unique aspects of your restaurant. Visual content is highly shareable and captures attention.
- **Engage with Your Audience:** Actively engage with your audience on social media. Respond to comments, ask questions, and encourage user-generated content. Social media is a two-way conversation, and building a community around your brand enhances its impact.
- **Utilize Influencer Marketing:** Collaborate with influencers in the food and lifestyle space to expand your reach. Influencers can provide authentic endorsements and expose your restaurant to a broader audience. Choose influencers whose values align with your brand.
- **Paid Advertising:** Explore paid advertising on social media platforms to target specific demographics and promote special events or promotions. Paid ads can enhance visibility and drive traffic to your restaurant.
- **Optimize Your Website:** Ensure that your website is user-friendly, visually appealing, and optimized for search engines. A well-designed website serves as a digital storefront and provides essential information such as menus, contact details, and reservations.
- **Email Marketing:** Build and nurture an email list to stay connected with your audience. Use email marketing to share updates, promotions, and exclusive offers. Personalized and targeted email campaigns can drive customer retention.

By embracing digital channels, you transform your restaurant into a dynamic and accessible culinary destination, fostering engagement and loyalty among a tech-savvy audience.

Customer Loyalty Programs: Cultivating Long-Term Relationships
Nurturing Relationships: Customer Loyalty Programs

Building a strong brand goes beyond attracting new guests; it involves cultivating lasting relationships with your existing customer base. Loyalty programs are powerful tools for retaining customers and encouraging repeat business. Consider the following elements when implementing a customer loyalty program:

- **Tiered Loyalty Programs:** Create tiered loyalty programs that offer escalating rewards based on customer loyalty. This encourages repeat visits and provides incentives for customers to move up the loyalty ladder.
- **Points-Based Systems:** Implement points-based systems where customers earn points for every purchase. These points can be redeemed for discounts, free items, or exclusive experiences. The accumulation of points serves as a tangible reward for loyalty.
- **Exclusive Offers and Promotions:** Provide exclusive offers and promotions to loyalty program members. This could include early access to new menu items, special event invitations, or members-only discounts. Exclusive perks enhance the sense of belonging.
- **Personalized Rewards:** Tailor rewards based on customer preferences and behavior. Personalized rewards demonstrate that you value and understand your customers, creating a more meaningful connection.
- **Anniversary and Birthday Rewards:** Recognize and celebrate important milestones with your customers. Offering special rewards or discounts on their anniversary of joining the loyalty program or on their birthday adds a personal touch.
- **Mobile Apps and Digital Loyalty Cards:** Explore mobile apps or digital loyalty cards that make it easy for customers to track their rewards and access exclusive offers. Digital loyalty programs enhance convenience and accessibility.
- **Promote Referral Programs:** Encourage your loyal customers to become brand ambassadors by referring friends and family. Implement referral programs that reward both the existing customer and the new customer, creating a positive cycle of growth.

Chapter 6: Menu Development: Crafting Culinary Excellence

In the intricate tapestry of restaurant management, menu development stands as a cornerstone, influencing the guest experience and shaping the identity of your culinary venture. This chapter explores the art of creating a balanced and appealing menu, implementing pricing strategies for profitability, and addressing dietary trends and preferences. By mastering these aspects, you elevate your restaurant's culinary offerings to an art form that captivates and satisfies your diverse audience.

Creating a Balanced and Appealing Menu: The Culinary Symphony
Harmony on the Plate: Crafting a Balanced Menu

A well-crafted menu is akin to a symphony, where each dish contributes to a harmonious and memorable dining experience. Consider the following elements when creating a balanced and appealing menu:

- **Diverse Culinary Offerings:** Provide a diverse range of culinary offerings to cater to varying tastes and preferences. Consider incorporating appetizers, main courses, desserts, and beverages that offer a balance of flavors, textures, and culinary styles.
- **Seasonal and Local Ingredients:** Embrace the freshness and vibrancy of seasonal and local ingredients. Highlighting these elements not only enhances the flavor profile of your dishes but also aligns with sustainability trends and supports local producers.
- **Menu Categories and Flow:** Organize your menu into logical categories, such as appetizers, entrees, and desserts. Ensure a smooth flow that guides the guest through a culinary journey. Consider grouping dishes based on shared themes or ingredients.
- **Vegetarian and Vegan Options:** Accommodate dietary preferences by offering a variety of vegetarian and vegan options. Highlighting plant-based dishes not only caters to a growing demographic but also adds diversity to your culinary repertoire.
- **Signature Dishes:** Showcase signature dishes that define your culinary identity. These could be unique creations or perfected renditions of classic favorites. Signature dishes contribute to brand recognition and guest loyalty.
- **Allergen Information:** Clearly communicate allergen information on the menu. Guests with dietary restrictions or allergies appreciate transparent information that allows them to make informed choices.
- **Visual Presentation:** Invest in visually appealing menu design. High-quality images, concise descriptions, and an aesthetically pleasing layout enhance the dining experience and contribute to the overall ambiance of your restaurant.

By carefully curating your menu to offer a symphony of flavors and experiences, you create a culinary journey that resonates with guests and keeps them coming back for more.

Pricing Strategies and Profitability: The Financial Ballet
Economic Choreography: Implementing Pricing Strategies

Pricing is a delicate dance between covering costs, ensuring profitability, and offering value to guests. Implementing effective pricing strategies requires a nuanced approach. Consider the following elements:

- **Cost-Based Pricing:** Begin by calculating the cost of ingredients, labor, overhead, and other expenses associated with each dish. Cost-based pricing ensures that menu prices cover your expenses while providing a reasonable profit margin.
- **Competitor Analysis:** Research the pricing strategies of competitors in your market. Understanding the price points of similar establishments helps you

position your restaurant competitively. Consider factors such as portion size, ingredients, and overall dining experience.
- **Value-Based Pricing:** Evaluate the perceived value of your dishes from the guest's perspective. Consider factors such as uniqueness, quality of ingredients, and the overall dining experience. Price dishes based on the value they offer to guests.
- **Bundle and Prix Fixe Options:** Introduce bundle options or prix fixe menus that offer a combination of dishes at a set price. This not only simplifies the decision-making process for guests but also encourages them to explore a variety of menu items.
- **Dynamic Pricing for Specials:** Implement dynamic pricing for special items or limited-time offerings. This creates a sense of exclusivity and urgency, encouraging guests to try new and seasonal dishes.
- **Strategic Placement:** Strategically place higher-margin items or signature dishes in prominent positions on the menu. Highlighting these items can influence guest choices and contribute to overall profitability.
- **Regular Menu Reviews:** Conduct regular reviews of your menu to assess the performance of each dish. Identify underperforming items and either adjust their pricing or consider reimagining the dish to enhance its appeal.

Balancing affordability with profitability is a nuanced art. By implementing thoughtful pricing strategies, you ensure that your restaurant remains financially sustainable while delivering value to your guests.

Addressing Dietary Trends and Preferences: The Culinary Mosaic
Culinary Adaptability: Navigating Dietary Trends

The modern dining landscape is characterized by diverse dietary trends and preferences. Adapting to these trends not only broadens your customer base but also positions your restaurant as responsive to evolving culinary expectations. Consider the following strategies:

- **Gluten-Free and Allergen-Friendly Options:** Offer a selection of gluten-free and allergen-friendly dishes. Clearly label these options on the menu to assist guests with dietary restrictions. This inclusivity enhances the dining experience for a broader audience.
- **Plant-Based and Vegan Choices:** Embrace the rising demand for plant-based and vegan options. Develop creative and flavorful plant-based dishes that cater to vegetarians and vegans. Highlighting these options contributes to a more inclusive and sustainable menu.
- **Low-Carb and Keto-Friendly Selections:** Consider incorporating low-carb and keto-friendly selections for guests adhering to these dietary lifestyles. These options provide alternatives for those seeking reduced carbohydrate intake.

- **Customization and Flexibility:** Design your menu to allow for customization. Providing flexibility in ingredient choices or preparation methods accommodates individual preferences and dietary needs. This personalized approach enhances the guest experience.
- **Ethnic and Global Influences:** Integrate global and ethnic

Chapter 7: Staff Management: Nurturing a Positive and Productive Work Environment

In the dynamic world of restaurant management, the success of your culinary venture hinges on effective staff management. This chapter delves into key aspects of staff management, including hiring and training staff, fostering employee motivation and retention, and addressing conflict resolution and team building. By prioritizing the well-being and development of your staff, you cultivate a positive and cohesive team that contributes to the overall success of your restaurant.

Hiring and Training Staff: Building the Foundation
Crafting Your Culinary Team: Hiring and Training

The process of building a successful restaurant starts with assembling a skilled and motivated team. Effective hiring and training practices are crucial elements of this foundation. Consider the following strategies:

- **Define Roles Clearly:** Clearly define the roles and responsibilities of each position within your restaurant. This includes front-of-house staff, kitchen staff, managerial roles, and any specialized positions. Clarity in job descriptions aids in the hiring process.
- **Cultural Fit:** Prioritize cultural fit during the hiring process. Assess whether potential candidates align with the values, ethos, and work culture of your restaurant. A cohesive team culture contributes to a positive work environment.
- **Thorough Interview Process:** Conduct thorough interviews to assess not only the candidate's skills and experience but also their interpersonal skills and attitude. Consider incorporating practical assessments or trial shifts to evaluate on-the-job performance.
- **Onboarding Process:** Develop a comprehensive onboarding process for new hires. This includes orientation sessions, introductions to team members, and detailed training on job responsibilities, safety protocols, and restaurant policies.
- **Continuous Training:** Implement ongoing training programs to enhance the skills and knowledge of your staff. This could involve cross-training employees for versatility, providing professional development opportunities, and staying current with industry trends.

- **Mentorship Programs:** Establish mentorship programs where experienced team members guide and support new hires. Mentorship fosters a sense of belonging and accelerates the integration of new employees into the team.
- **Communication Channels:** Create open channels of communication for staff to express concerns, provide feedback, and seek clarification. Effective communication is essential for a collaborative and informed team.

By investing time and effort into the hiring and training process, you lay the groundwork for a skilled and cohesive team that contributes to the success of your restaurant.

Employee Motivation and Retention: Cultivating a Positive Work Culture
Nurturing Talent: Employee Motivation and Retention

Employee motivation and retention are critical factors in maintaining a stable and high-performing team. A positive work culture and proactive measures contribute to employee satisfaction and longevity. Consider the following strategies:

- **Recognition and Appreciation:** Acknowledge and appreciate the efforts of your staff. Regularly recognize achievements, milestones, and exceptional performance. This can be done through verbal praise, employee of the month programs, or small incentives.
- **Competitive Compensation:** Ensure that your staff receives competitive compensation within the industry standards. Regularly review and adjust wages to reflect market trends and to show that you value the contributions of your team.
- **Opportunities for Advancement:** Provide opportunities for career growth and advancement within your restaurant. Establish clear paths for progression, and offer training and support for employees seeking to take on more responsibilities.
- **Work-Life Balance:** Strive to maintain a healthy work-life balance for your staff. Implement reasonable working hours, consider flexible scheduling options, and provide adequate breaks. A well-balanced lifestyle contributes to employee satisfaction.
- **Employee Benefits:** Consider offering additional benefits such as health insurance, retirement plans, or meal discounts. Comprehensive benefits contribute to the overall well-being of your staff and demonstrate a commitment to their welfare.
- **Regular Feedback and Check-Ins:** Conduct regular performance reviews and check-ins with your staff. Provide constructive feedback, discuss career goals, and address any concerns or challenges. Two-way communication fosters a sense of partnership.
- **Team Building Activities:** Organize team-building activities and events to strengthen interpersonal relationships and camaraderie. This could include

outings, workshops, or collaborative projects. A cohesive team is more resilient and productive.
- **Flexible Scheduling:** Consider implementing flexible scheduling options to accommodate the diverse needs and preferences of your staff. This flexibility promotes a supportive work environment.

By prioritizing employee motivation and retention, you create a work culture that attracts and retains top talent, contributing to the stability and success of your restaurant.

Delegating Tasks to Employees: The Art of Empowerment

In the intricate ballet of restaurant management, mastering the art of delegation is a fundamental skill that not only lightens the load for managers but also empowers employees, fostering motivation and enhanced performance. This chapter explores the nuances of delegating tasks, providing insights into the manager's approach and delving into the transformative effects delegation can have on employee motivation and overall performance.

The Manager's Approach to Delegating Tasks: Crafting a Symphony of Efficiency
Orchestrating Productivity: The Manager's Role in Delegation

Effective delegation is not merely a matter of assigning tasks; it is a strategic orchestration of skills, responsibilities, and empowerment. As a manager, adopting the right approach is instrumental in creating an environment where delegation becomes a catalyst for success. Consider the following strategies:

- **Understanding Individual Strengths:** Before delegating tasks, take the time to understand the unique strengths and skills of each team member. Recognizing individual capabilities allows for more targeted task assignments, maximizing efficiency and job satisfaction.
- **Clear Communication:** Articulate expectations clearly when assigning tasks. Provide a detailed explanation of the task, its objectives, and any specific requirements. Open a channel for questions and ensure that the employee feels comfortable seeking clarification.
- **Matching Tasks to Skills:** Delegate tasks based on employees' skills and strengths. Matching tasks to individuals not only ensures a higher likelihood of success but also provides an opportunity for skill development and growth.
- **Encouraging Autonomy:** Empower employees by giving them autonomy in completing assigned tasks. Trusting your team members fosters a sense of ownership and responsibility, encouraging them to take pride in their work.
- **Setting Realistic Goals:** Establish realistic and achievable goals for delegated tasks. Unrealistic expectations can lead to frustration and demotivation. Setting attainable objectives creates a positive environment where employees can thrive.
- **Providing Resources and Support:** Ensure that employees have the necessary resources and support to carry out delegated tasks successfully.

This may include access to information, training, or additional manpower. A well-supported team is a more productive team.
- **Establishing Accountability:** Clearly define roles and responsibilities, including deadlines and milestones. Establishing accountability ensures that employees understand the importance of their contributions and the impact on the overall success of the restaurant.
- **Feedback and Recognition:** Provide constructive feedback on completed tasks. Acknowledge a job well done and offer guidance for improvement when necessary. Recognizing achievements reinforces positive behavior and encourages continuous growth.

By approaching delegation with a strategic mindset, managers become architects of efficiency, leveraging the strengths of their team to create a harmonious workplace.

Delegating Tasks for Employee Motivation and Performance: Empowering Excellence

Unlocking Potential: The Motivational Power of Delegation

Beyond the practicalities of task distribution, delegation carries profound implications for employee motivation and performance. When done thoughtfully, delegation transforms routine tasks into opportunities for growth and empowerment. Consider the following ways in which delegation becomes a motivational force:

- **Fostering a Sense of Trust:** Delegating tasks communicates a fundamental trust in the abilities of your team members. This trust, when reciprocated, establishes a positive and collaborative relationship between managers and employees.
- **Skill Development and Growth Opportunities:** Delegating tasks that align with employees' skills but also stretch their capabilities fosters continuous learning and skill development. Offering growth opportunities motivates employees to invest in their professional development.
- **Enhancing Job Satisfaction:** Employees who feel trusted, valued, and challenged in their roles are more likely to experience higher job satisfaction. Delegating meaningful tasks contributes to a sense of purpose and fulfillment in the workplace.
- **Promoting Ownership and Responsibility:** Delegating tasks empowers employees to take ownership of their work. When individuals feel a sense of responsibility for the tasks assigned to them, they are more likely to approach their work with dedication and commitment.
- **Increasing Engagement and Morale:** Engagement and morale flourish in an environment where employees are actively involved in their work. Delegating tasks provides a platform for meaningful contribution, leading to higher levels of engagement and overall morale.

- **Building a Culture of Collaboration:** Delegation encourages a collaborative culture where team members support each other in achieving shared goals. As employees work together on delegated tasks, they build a sense of camaraderie and unity.
- **Recognition for Contributions:** Acknowledging the significance of delegated tasks and recognizing employees for their contributions is a powerful motivational tool. Publicly recognizing achievements, whether big or small, reinforces a culture of appreciation.
- **Reducing Burnout and Stress:** Strategic delegation prevents burnout by distributing workload evenly among team members. Avoiding excessive workload on a few individuals promotes a healthier work-life balance, reducing stress and enhancing overall well-being.

In essence, delegation becomes a motivational catalyst when it transforms routine tasks into avenues for professional growth, personal development, and a profound sense of purpose.

Case Studies in Delegation: Realizing the Impact
Stories of Success: How Delegation Transforms Performance

Let's explore two hypothetical scenarios illustrating the transformative impact of delegation on employee motivation and performance.

Case Study 1: Emma's Culinary Innovation
Emma, a talented sous chef, has consistently showcased creativity in her approach to culinary creations. Recognizing her potential, the head chef decides to delegate the planning and execution of a special menu for an upcoming event to Emma.

Result:

- **Motivation:** Emma feels a surge of motivation as she takes on this significant responsibility. She is excited about the opportunity to showcase her skills and contribute to the restaurant's success.
- **Performance:** The special menu is a hit, receiving positive feedback from guests. Emma's performance exceeds expectations, and the sense of accomplishment propels her to explore further culinary innovations.

Case Study 2: Carlos Takes the Lead in Customer Service
Carlos, a front-of-house staff member, has shown a natural flair for customer service. The restaurant manager decides to delegate the responsibility of implementing a new customer feedback system and training the team on enhanced service techniques to Carlos.

Result:

- **Motivation:** Carlos is motivated by the trust placed in him to lead initiatives that directly impact customer satisfaction. He sees this delegation as an opportunity to further hone his leadership and customer service skills.

- **Performance:** The new customer feedback system is successfully implemented, leading to improved customer satisfaction scores. Carlos's proactive approach in training the team contributes to a more polished and customer-focused service.

These case studies highlight how strategic delegation can unlock the potential within team members, leading to heightened motivation, improved performance, and a positive impact on the overall success of the restaurant.

Chapter 8: Overcoming Challenges in Delegation: A Manager's Guide
Navigating Obstacles: Strategies for Effective Delegation

While delegation holds immense potential for employee motivation and performance, it is not without challenges. Managers may encounter resistance, communication barriers, or concerns about relinquishing control. Here are strategies for overcoming common challenges:

- **Communication Breakdowns:** To avoid misunderstandings, ensure clear and open communication when delegating tasks. Provide detailed instructions, encourage questions, and establish a feedback loop to address concerns promptly.
- **Resistance to Delegation:** Some employees may resist taking on additional responsibilities due to concerns about workload or self-doubt. Address resistance by emphasizing the growth opportunities and the trust placed in their abilities.
- **Fear of Micromanagement:** Employees may fear that delegation comes with excessive oversight. Clarify

Conflict Resolution and Team Building: Fostering Collaboration
Navigating Challenges: Conflict Resolution and Team Building

In any workplace, conflicts may arise, and effective conflict resolution is crucial for maintaining a positive and productive environment. Additionally, proactive team-building efforts contribute to a cohesive and collaborative work culture. Consider the following strategies:

- **Open Communication Channels:** Establish open and transparent communication channels for addressing conflicts. Encourage staff to voice concerns or grievances and provide a platform for constructive discussions.
- **Mediation and Conflict Resolution Training:** Invest in training for managers and key staff members on conflict resolution and mediation techniques. Equip your team with the skills to address and resolve conflicts in a fair and impartial manner.
- **Address Issues Promptly:** Act promptly to address conflicts or interpersonal issues within the team. Timely intervention prevents escalation and

Adapting to Challenges: Navigating Crises and Changing Consumer Behaviors

In the ever-evolving landscape of restaurant management, adaptability is a cornerstone for success. This chapter explores strategies for managing crises, particularly in the context of pandemics, and addresses the importance of adapting to changing consumer behaviors. By embracing flexibility and innovation, you position your restaurant to weather challenges and thrive in dynamic environments.

Accountability in Restaurant Management: Nurturing a Culture of Responsibility

In the intricate tapestry of restaurant management, accountability stands as a linchpin for success. This chapter delves into the critical role of accountability, examining its significance for both managers and owners. The exploration includes insights into fostering a fair accountability system, the impact on employee performance, and real-world scenarios showcasing the transformative power of responsibility in the restaurant setting.

Ego-Free Transactions: Nurturing Harmony in Restaurant Management

In the intricate dance of restaurant management, success often hinges on the ability of owners and managers to leave their egos at the door. This chapter explores the transformative power of ego-free transactions, illuminating how cultivating humility and empathy can foster harmonious relationships across all facets of the restaurant ecosystem. From interactions between owners and managers to dealings with employees, distributors, and co-workers, adopting an ego-free approach becomes a cornerstone for building a resilient and collaborative restaurant culture.

Chapter 9: The Pitfall of Ego in Restaurant Management: Breaking Down the Barriers
Ego as a Barrier: A Hindrance to Effective Transactions

In the fast-paced world of restaurant management, where decisions are swift, and pressures are high, the presence of unchecked egos can act as a formidable barrier. Ego-driven interactions can manifest in various ways, such as:

- **Power Struggles:** Ego clashes between owners and managers can lead to power struggles, hindering effective decision-making and collaboration.
- **Communication Breakdowns:** An inflated ego can obstruct clear communication, leading to misunderstandings, conflicts, and a breakdown in team cohesion.
- **Resistance to Feedback:** Ego-centric individuals may be resistant to feedback, hindering growth and improvement at both the individual and organizational levels.
- **Strained Employee Relations:** Employees may perceive an ego-driven management style as authoritarian or unapproachable, leading to strained relationships and diminished morale.

- **Disrupted Collaborations:** Ego clashes among co-workers or with external partners, such as distributors, can disrupt collaborations, impacting the overall efficiency and success of the restaurant.

The Transformative Power of Humility: An Ego-Free Approach
Embracing Humility: Building Bridges in Restaurant Management

Humility serves as the antidote to ego-driven challenges, offering a pathway to more effective and meaningful transactions. Embracing humility in restaurant management involves:

- **Open-minded Decision-Making:** Humility enables owners and managers to approach decisions with an open mind, considering diverse perspectives and fostering collaborative problem-solving.
- **Active Listening:** Practicing humility involves active listening, a skill crucial for understanding the needs, concerns, and suggestions of team members, co-workers, and external partners.
- **Embracing Constructive Feedback:** A humble approach encourages a receptiveness to constructive feedback, promoting continuous improvement and personal growth.
- **Cultivating Empathy:** Humility fosters empathy, allowing owners and managers to relate to the experiences and challenges faced by employees, co-workers, and external collaborators.
- **Acknowledging Mistakes:** Humility involves acknowledging mistakes and learning from them. This openness to self-reflection contributes to a culture of accountability and transparency.
- **Sharing Successes:** Humble leaders attribute successes to the collective efforts of the team, recognizing and celebrating the contributions of everyone involved.
- **Building Trust:** Humility builds trust among team members, creating an environment where individuals feel comfortable sharing ideas, concerns, and feedback without fear of judgment.

Owner-Manager Dynamics: Fostering Collaboration, Not Conflict
Navigating Ego Dynamics: Strategies for Owner-Manager Interactions

In the owner-manager relationship, ego dynamics can either foster collaboration or breed conflict. Strategies for cultivating an ego-free approach include:

- **Clearly Defined Roles and Expectations:** Clearly define the roles and expectations of owners and managers. This clarity minimizes potential power struggles by establishing a framework for collaboration.
- **Regular Communication:** Foster open and regular communication between owners and managers. This includes scheduled meetings, check-ins, and an open-door policy to encourage transparent dialogue.

- **Shared Decision-Making:** Embrace shared decision-making processes where input from both owners and managers is valued. This collaborative approach promotes a sense of ownership and shared responsibility.
- **Recognition of Contributions:** Acknowledge and recognize the contributions of both owners and managers. A culture of appreciation fosters mutual respect and minimizes the potential for ego-driven conflicts.
- **Conflict Resolution Protocols:** Establish protocols for conflict resolution that prioritize open communication and mediation. Having a structured approach to addressing conflicts prevents them from escalating.
- **Leadership Training:** Provide leadership training for both owners and managers, emphasizing the importance of humility, empathy, and effective communication in building a harmonious working relationship.
- **Setting a Cultural Tone:** Owners play a crucial role in setting the cultural tone of the restaurant. By embodying humility and a collaborative spirit, owners set an example for the entire team.

Employee Interactions: Nurturing a Supportive Environment
Ego-Free Employee Transactions: Strategies for Supportive Interactions

Owners and managers, as leaders, have a direct impact on the workplace environment and employee experiences. Strategies for fostering ego-free interactions with employees include:

- **Approachable Leadership:** Cultivate an approachable leadership style. Employees should feel comfortable approaching owners and managers with concerns, suggestions, or feedback.
- **Active Listening Sessions:** Schedule regular active listening sessions where owners and managers actively seek input from employees. This creates a platform for open communication and ensures that employee perspectives are valued.
- **Recognition and Appreciation:** Recognize and appreciate the contributions of employees. Publicly acknowledging their efforts fosters a positive culture and minimizes feelings of being overlooked.
- **Promoting Team Collaboration:** Encourage a collaborative team environment where every member feels valued. Minimize hierarchical barriers that may inhibit open communication and collaboration.
- **Transparency in Decision-Making:** When possible, be transparent about decision-making processes that may impact employees. This transparency builds trust and helps employees understand the rationale behind certain decisions.
- **Employee Training and Development:** Invest in the training and development of employees. This demonstrates a commitment to their growth and contributes to a positive, ego-free workplace culture.

- **Conflict Resolution Resources:** Provide resources and mechanisms for employees to address conflicts or concerns. An established process for conflict resolution ensures that issues are addressed promptly and fairly.

Distributor and Co-worker Collaborations: Navigating Ego Challenges
Creating a Collaborative Ecosystem: Strategies for External Interactions

Interactions with external partners, such as distributors and co-workers, also benefit from an ego-free approach. Strategies include:

- **Building Positive Vendor Relationships:** Cultivate positive relationships with distributors by fostering open communication, clear expectations, and a shared commitment to mutual success.
- **Team Collaboration with Co-workers:** Encourage collaboration among co-workers by minimizing competition and promoting a culture where everyone's contributions are valued.
- **Negotiation without Ego:** When negotiating terms with distributors or co-workers, focus on mutual benefit rather than asserting dominance. Negotiate with a collaborative spirit to foster long-term partnerships.
- **Conflict Resolution Protocols:** Establish clear protocols for resolving conflicts with external partners. Transparent communication and fair conflict resolution processes contribute to a healthy working relationship.
- **Cross-Functional Collaboration:** Facilitate cross-functional collaboration between different departments or teams within the restaurant. Breaking down silos encourages a more integrated and collaborative working environment.
- **Recognition of External Contributions:** Recognize and appreciate the contributions of external partners. Whether it's a distributor going the extra mile or a co-worker collaborating seamlessly, acknowledging their efforts strengthens relationships.

Case Studies: Ego-Free Transformations in Action
Real-World Scenarios: The Impact of Ego-Free Transactions

Explore two hypothetical scenarios showcasing the transformative impact of ego-free transactions:

Case Study 1: Owner-Manager Collaboration
Sarah, a restaurant owner, recognizes the importance of an ego-free approach in her collaboration with the general manager, Alex. They establish clear roles, communicate openly, and share decision-making responsibilities. The result is a harmonious working relationship that filters down to the entire team.

Outcome:

- **Effective Decision-Making:** The collaborative approach leads to more effective decision-making, benefiting the overall efficiency of the restaurant.

- **Positive Team Culture:** The positive owner-manager dynamic sets a tone of collaboration that permeates the entire team, fostering a positive and supportive culture.

Case Study 2: Ego-Free Employee Engagement
John, a manager, actively practices humility in his interactions with employees. He listens actively, acknowledges their contributions, and provides opportunities for growth. This ego-free approach leads to increased employee engagement, higher morale, and a more cohesive team.

Outcome:

- **Employee Morale Boost:** Employees feel valued and appreciated, resulting in higher morale and job satisfaction.
- **Productivity and Collaboration:** The ego-free environment encourages collaboration and innovation, contributing to increased productivity within the team.

Overcoming Challenges: Strategies for Sustaining Ego-Free Transactions
Addressing Common Hurdles: A Roadmap to Sustained Ego-Free Transactions

While embracing an ego-free approach brings numerous benefits, challenges may arise. Strategies for overcoming common hurdles include:

- **Leadership Training Programs:** Implement ongoing leadership training programs that emphasize the importance of humility, effective communication, and collaboration.
- **Cultivating a Learning Culture:** Foster a culture of continuous learning where owners, managers, and employees are encouraged to seek personal and professional growth.
- **Regular Check-Ins:** Schedule regular check-ins to assess the health of relationships within the restaurant ecosystem. This proactive approach allows for the identification and resolution of potential issues before they escalate.
- **360-Degree Feedback Mechanisms:** Establish 360-degree feedback mechanisms that allow individuals at all levels to provide constructive feedback. This inclusive approach ensures that everyone's perspectives are considered.
- **Conflict Resolution Resources:** Provide accessible resources for conflict resolution, both internally and externally. Transparent and fair conflict resolution processes contribute to a healthy and respectful working environment.
- **Commitment to Continuous Improvement:** Emphasize a commitment to continuous improvement at all levels of the organization. This commitment reinforces the idea that everyone plays a role in the collective success of the restaurant.

Conclusion: Cultivating a Culture of Collaboration and Respect
The Journey Forward: Ego-Free Transactions as a Guiding Philosophy

In the tapestry of restaurant management, the philosophy of ego-free transactions emerges as a guiding principle for success. Owners, managers, employees, distributors, and co-workers—all contribute to the intricate dance of daily operations. By embracing humility, empathy, and open communication, stakeholders can navigate challenges, foster collaboration, and build a resilient and thriving restaurant culture.

As the restaurant industry evolves and faces new challenges, the importance of ego-free transactions becomes even more pronounced. It is not just a philosophy; it is a commitment to creating a workplace where individuals can flourish, contribute their best, and collectively shape the success of the restaurant. Through ego-free interactions, the restaurant becomes not only a place for culinary excellence but also a haven for collaboration, respect, and shared achievements.

Chapter 10: The Manager's Role in Accountability: Orchestrating Excellence

Leadership Accountability: Setting the Tone

Accountability in restaurant management begins at the top, with managers playing a pivotal role in establishing and reinforcing a culture of responsibility. The manager's approach to accountability sets the tone for the entire team. Consider the following strategies for effective leadership accountability:

- **Lead by Example:** Managers must exemplify the standards of accountability they expect from their team. Demonstrating a strong work ethic, adherence to policies, and a commitment to excellence establishes a foundation for a responsible workplace culture.
- **Clear Communication of Expectations:** Articulate expectations clearly, both in terms of individual and team responsibilities. Ensure that employees understand their roles, goals, and the broader objectives of the restaurant. Clear communication minimizes ambiguity and sets the stage for accountability.
- **Establishing Measurable Objectives:** Define measurable objectives and key performance indicators (KPIs) for both individuals and the team. Establishing benchmarks provides a basis for evaluating performance and holding employees accountable for specific outcomes.
- **Feedback and Recognition:** Implement a feedback system that includes regular performance reviews and constructive feedback. Recognize and acknowledge achievements, providing positive reinforcement for accountability and dedication to excellence.
- **Empowerment Through Responsibility:** Delegate responsibilities to team members, empowering them to take ownership of specific tasks. This not only distributes the workload but also instills a sense of pride and accountability in contributing to the success of the restaurant.

- **Problem-Solving Approach:** Encourage a problem-solving mindset among your team. When issues arise, promote a collaborative approach to finding solutions rather than placing blame. A solution-oriented culture fosters a sense of collective accountability.
- **Consistency in Accountability Measures:** Apply accountability measures consistently across all team members. Consistency reinforces fairness and prevents perceptions of favoritism. It also ensures that everyone is held to the same standards.
- **Training and Development Opportunities:** Invest in the training and development of your team. Providing opportunities for skill enhancement not only improves performance but also communicates a commitment to the professional growth of your employees.

By embodying a strong sense of accountability, managers lay the groundwork for a culture where responsibility becomes a shared value, propelling the restaurant towards operational excellence.

Chapter 11: The Owner's Responsibility: Cultivating a Culture of Accountability

Owner's Oversight: Aligning Vision and Accountability

Owners bear the responsibility of shaping the overarching vision and values of the restaurant. In doing so, they play a vital role in cultivating a culture of accountability that permeates every aspect of the establishment. Consider the following strategies for owners to foster accountability:

- **Define Core Values:** Clearly define the core values that underpin the restaurant's identity. These values serve as a compass for decision-making and behavior, fostering a sense of purpose and accountability among employees.
- **Alignment of Vision:** Ensure that the vision for the restaurant aligns with the values and goals set by the ownership. When employees perceive a cohesive vision, they are more likely to feel connected to the overarching objectives, fostering a sense of accountability.
- **Investment in Resources:** Owners must invest in the resources required for employee success. This includes providing adequate training, modern equipment, and a conducive work environment. A well-equipped team is better positioned to meet and exceed expectations.
- **Transparency in Communication:** Maintain open lines of communication with employees. Transparency about the restaurant's performance, challenges, and future plans instills trust and a collective sense of responsibility in achieving shared goals.
- **Recognition of Employee Contributions:** Acknowledge and celebrate the contributions of employees to the success of the restaurant. Recognizing the

efforts of individuals reinforces the importance of their roles and encourages continued commitment to accountability.
- **Investigation of Performance Metrics:** Regularly assess performance metrics and key indicators. Owners should actively participate in evaluating the success of the restaurant and use data-driven insights to guide decisions and strategies.
- **Accessibility to Ownership:** Create an environment where employees feel comfortable approaching ownership with concerns, ideas, or feedback. Accessibility fosters a collaborative atmosphere and reinforces a sense of shared responsibility in achieving the restaurant's objectives.
- **Inclusion in Decision-Making:** Include employees in certain decision-making processes, especially those that directly impact their roles. Seeking input and involving the team in relevant decisions fosters a sense of ownership and accountability for the outcomes.

Owners, as stewards of the restaurant's vision, hold the power to shape a culture of accountability that permeates every level of the organization.

Accountability and Employee Performance: A Symbiotic Relationship
The Performance Paradigm: Flourishing Through Accountability

The interplay between accountability and employee performance is dynamic and symbiotic. When accountability is cultivated and embraced, it becomes a catalyst for elevated performance. Consider the ways in which accountability contributes to enhanced employee performance:

- **Clarity of Expectations:** Accountability provides employees with a clear understanding of what is expected of them. When expectations are communicated and understood, individuals are better equipped to align their efforts with organizational goals, driving improved performance.
- **Motivation through Ownership:** Accountability creates a sense of ownership over one's responsibilities. When employees feel a personal stake in their tasks, they are inherently motivated to excel, contributing to heightened performance and a dedication to achieving excellence.
- **Goal Alignment:** Establishing measurable objectives and KPIs ensures that employees' goals are aligned with the broader objectives of the restaurant. This alignment provides a framework for focused and purposeful efforts, leading to improved performance outcomes.
- **Feedback for Growth:** A culture of accountability emphasizes constructive feedback. Regular performance reviews and feedback sessions provide employees with insights into their strengths and areas for improvement, guiding them towards continuous growth and development.
- **Responsibility as a Source of Pride:** Being entrusted with responsibilities fosters a sense of pride among employees. This pride serves as a powerful

motivator, inspiring individuals to perform at their best to uphold the trust placed in them.
- **Problem-Solving Aptitude:** An accountable workforce is more likely to approach challenges with a problem-solving mindset. When individuals take responsibility for finding solutions, it leads to increased innovation, adaptability, and resilience in the face of obstacles.
- **Team Collaboration:** Accountability encourages collaboration and mutual support within a team. When every team member is committed to their responsibilities, the collective performance of the team is elevated, resulting in a more cohesive and high-performing unit.
- **Adaptability to Change:** Accountable employees are more adaptable to change. They embrace new responsibilities and challenges with a proactive mindset, contributing to a culture of continuous improvement and a workforce that thrives in dynamic environments.

Through the symbiotic relationship between accountability and performance, a restaurant transforms into a dynamic and high-achieving organization.

Chapter 12: Direct Communication with Employees: Bridging Gaps in Ownership Insight

In the intricate dynamics of restaurant management, direct communication between owners and employees can be a transformative approach, unveiling insights that might otherwise remain hidden in the shadows. This chapter explores the significance of owners engaging directly with employees, bypassing potential barriers erected by middle management. Through candid conversations and firsthand interactions, owners can gain invaluable perspectives, foster a culture of transparency, and navigate the nuanced landscape of their restaurant with a clearer understanding.

The Challenge of Information Filtering: Bypassing Managerial Filters
Navigating Communication Channels: A Case for Direct Owner-Employee Interaction

In the hierarchical structure of restaurant management, information often undergoes a series of filters before reaching the owner. Managers, acting as intermediaries, play a crucial role in shaping the narrative that eventually reaches the top. However, this well-intentioned filtering can inadvertently lead to information distortion or omissions.

Managerial Filters: A Double-Edged Sword
While managers are essential for day-to-day operations and communication, their role as filters can pose challenges:
- **Protective Instincts:** Managers, seeking to protect their positions or avoid confrontation, may filter information to present a more favorable picture. This protective instinct, while natural, can result in owners being shielded from critical feedback or issues.

- **Selective Reporting:** Managers might unconsciously engage in selective reporting, emphasizing positive aspects and downplaying challenges. This can create a skewed perception of the restaurant's performance, hindering the owner's ability to make informed decisions.
- **Fear of Reprisal:** Employees, on the other hand, may be hesitant to share certain concerns or feedback with managers, fearing reprisal or adverse consequences. This fear can create a communication barrier, preventing owners from understanding the full spectrum of issues within the restaurant.

Direct Owner-Employee Interaction: Unveiling Hidden Realities
Breaking the Chains: Benefits of Direct Communication

Engaging in direct conversations with employees offers owners a direct line to the heartbeat of their restaurant. This unfiltered approach yields several benefits:

- **Authentic Insights:** Direct communication allows owners to hear unfiltered, authentic insights directly from the source. Employees, unencumbered by hierarchical constraints, are more likely to share their genuine perspectives on various aspects of the restaurant.
- **Identification of Unaddressed Issues:** Owners, by circumventing managerial filters, can identify and address issues that may have been overlooked or deliberately filtered out. This proactive approach enables a quicker response to challenges and contributes to a more resilient and adaptive restaurant.
- **Building Trust and Transparency:** Direct communication fosters trust between owners and employees. When employees see that their voices are heard and valued, a culture of transparency is cultivated, promoting open dialogue and collaboration.
- **Empowerment of Employees:** Direct interaction empowers employees by providing them with a platform to express their ideas, concerns, and suggestions directly to the owner. This empowerment contributes to a sense of ownership and accountability among the workforce.
- **Real-time Feedback:** Owners gain access to real-time feedback on various aspects of the restaurant, from operational efficiency to employee morale. This immediacy allows for prompt decision-making and intervention, preventing issues from escalating.
- **Recognition of Employee Contributions:** Direct communication allows owners to personally acknowledge and recognize the contributions of employees. This recognition serves as a motivational tool, reinforcing positive behaviors and fostering a sense of pride among team members.

Strategies for Effective Owner-Employee Communication
Navigating Direct Conversations: Best Practices for Owners

While the benefits of direct communication are evident, engaging in meaningful conversations with employees requires a thoughtful and strategic approach. Consider the following best practices for owners:

- **Establishing Approachability:** Create an atmosphere where employees feel comfortable approaching the owner. This involves cultivating an approachable demeanor, actively listening, and demonstrating genuine interest in the perspectives of the workforce.
- **Scheduled Town Hall Meetings:** Organize regular town hall meetings or open forums where employees can share their thoughts and concerns directly with the owner. These sessions provide a structured platform for open communication and collective problem-solving.
- **Anonymous Feedback Mechanism:** Implement an anonymous feedback mechanism to encourage employees who might be hesitant to voice concerns openly. This can be through suggestion boxes, digital surveys, or other confidential channels.
- **Casual Informal Interactions:** Foster informal interactions by occasionally joining employees during breaks, engaging in casual conversations, or participating in team-building activities. These informal settings often encourage more candid communication.
- **Employee Recognition Programs:** Use direct communication to recognize and appreciate employee contributions. This can be done publicly during team meetings or through personalized notes and acknowledgments.
- **Listening Tours:** Periodically conduct listening tours where the owner actively seeks feedback and input from employees at all levels. This hands-on approach demonstrates a commitment to understanding the realities of the restaurant from the ground up.
- **Clear Communication Channels:** Ensure that communication channels are clear and accessible. Employees should know how to reach out to the owner, whether through designated time slots, email, or other established channels.
- **Response and Action:** Demonstrate responsiveness to the feedback received. When employees see that their input leads to tangible actions or improvements, it reinforces the value of direct communication and encourages ongoing engagement.

Case Studies: Stories of Impactful Direct Communication
Real-World Scenarios: How Direct Communication Reshapes Perceptions

Let's explore two hypothetical scenarios illustrating the transformative impact of direct owner-employee communication.

Case Study 1: Sarah's Insights on Service Improvement
Sarah, a server with a keen eye for customer service, has noticed a recurring issue in the dining experience that is not effectively communicated through the management

chain. The owner, during a scheduled town hall meeting, directly engages with Sarah and other front-of-house staff.

Result:

- **Authentic Feedback:** Sarah shares her observations directly with the owner, highlighting specific challenges in the service process.
- **Immediate Action:** The owner, impressed by Sarah's insights, implements changes to improve the identified service aspects, leading to enhanced customer satisfaction.
- **Cultural Impact:** Other employees witness the positive outcome of direct communication, fostering a culture of openness and collaboration.

Case Study 2: John's Suggestions for Operational Efficiency
John, a line cook, has innovative ideas for streamlining kitchen operations but feels hesitant to share them through regular channels. The owner, during a casual interaction in the kitchen, engages in conversation with John.

Result:

- **Creative Solutions:** John, feeling encouraged by the owner's approachability, shares his ideas for optimizing kitchen processes.
- **Implementation of Ideas:** The owner, recognizing the merit of John's suggestions, implements some of the proposed changes, resulting in increased efficiency.
- **Employee Empowerment:** John's experience encourages other employees to share their ideas, contributing to a culture of continuous improvement.

These case studies illustrate how direct communication opens channels for valuable insights, propelling positive changes within the restaurant.

Overcoming Challenges: Navigating Potential Pitfalls
Addressing Concerns: Strategies for Mitigating Challenges

While direct communication offers numerous benefits, potential challenges must be acknowledged and addressed. Consider strategies for mitigating common concerns:

- **Balancing Hierarchical Dynamics:** Navigate the hierarchical dynamics by emphasizing a collaborative and inclusive culture. Reinforce that direct communication is not about undermining managerial roles but rather about fostering transparency and collaboration.
- **Ensuring Consistency:** Maintain consistency in direct communication efforts. Avoid sporadic interactions that may lead to a perception of favoritism or tokenism. Consistency builds trust and reinforces the commitment to open dialogue.
- **Addressing Managerial Concerns:** Proactively address concerns from middle management about potential bypassing. Emphasize that direct

communication complements managerial roles and contributes to a more informed and engaged workforce.
- **Anonymous Feedback Channels:** Implement anonymous feedback channels to address concerns about potential reprisals. Anonymous mechanisms provide a safe space for employees to share sensitive or critical feedback without fear of consequences.
- **Communication Training:** Provide communication training for both owners and employees. This includes active listening skills, conflict resolution strategies, and fostering a positive communication culture.

Conclusion: Fostering a Culture of Openness and Collaboration
The Path Forward: Embracing Direct Communication as a Catalyst

Direct communication between owners and employees is a powerful catalyst for fostering a culture of openness, transparency, and collaboration within the restaurant. By actively engaging with the workforce, owners gain authentic insights, address concerns at their root, and contribute to a more resilient and adaptive organization.

As owners navigate the intricate landscape of restaurant management, the direct line of communication becomes a compass, guiding decisions, inspiring innovation, and shaping a shared vision for success. Embracing this approach not only transforms the restaurant into a dynamic and responsive entity but also strengthens the bonds between ownership and the invaluable individuals who contribute to its daily vibrancy—the employees.

Chapter 13: Strategies for Managing Crises: Navigating Uncharted Waters

Navigating the Storm: Crisis Management Strategies

The restaurant industry is no stranger to crises, and effective crisis management is essential for safeguarding your establishment during challenging times. Whether facing a pandemic, natural disaster, economic downturn, or other unforeseen events, consider the following strategies:

- **Develop a Crisis Management Plan:** Proactively develop a comprehensive crisis management plan that outlines protocols, responsibilities, and communication strategies. This plan should cover various scenarios, including health emergencies, supply chain disruptions, and economic challenges.
- **Clear Communication:** Transparent and timely communication is paramount during a crisis. Keep your staff, customers, and stakeholders informed about the situation, safety measures, and any changes in operations. Utilize multiple communication channels, including social media, email, and in-house signage.
- **Flexibility in Operations:** Be prepared to adapt your operations based on the nature of the crisis. This could involve adjusting hours, offering takeout and delivery services, implementing safety measures, or temporarily closing and reopening based on local guidelines.

- **Financial Planning:** Establish contingency plans for financial challenges. This may involve renegotiating contracts with suppliers, seeking financial assistance programs, or adjusting budgets to account for reduced revenue. Maintaining a financial cushion can help weather periods of economic uncertainty.
- **Staff Support:** Prioritize the well-being of your staff during crises. This includes providing clear guidance on safety measures, offering support for mental health, and, if necessary, implementing flexible work arrangements. A supportive approach fosters loyalty and resilience.
- **Adaptation of Marketing Strategies:** Adjust your marketing strategies to align with the current climate. This may involve emphasizing safety measures in your communications, offering promotions to boost sales, or leveraging digital marketing channels to reach customers staying at home.
- **Community Engagement:** Engage with the local community during challenging times. This could involve supporting local initiatives, collaborating with other businesses, or providing assistance to those in need. Building community ties fosters goodwill and resilience.

By proactively planning for crises and maintaining flexibility in your approach, you position your restaurant to navigate challenges and emerge stronger on the other side.

Adapting to Changing Consumer Behaviors: Embracing Evolution
Fluid Dynamics: Adapting to Shifting Consumer Behaviors

Consumer behaviors in the restaurant industry are subject to constant evolution, influenced by factors such as technological advancements, cultural shifts, and, as seen in recent times, global events like pandemics. Adapting to changing consumer behaviors is crucial for staying relevant and meeting the evolving needs of your audience. Consider the following strategies:

- **Embrace Technology:** The integration of technology in the dining experience is increasingly prevalent. Offer online ordering, delivery services, and mobile payment options to cater to tech-savvy consumers. Utilize reservation systems and loyalty apps to enhance customer engagement.
- **Focus on Health and Wellness:** Recent global events have heightened consumer awareness of health and wellness. Adapt your menu to include healthier options, clearly communicate hygiene and safety measures, and consider incorporating nutritional information into your menu.
- **Sustainability Initiatives:** Environmental consciousness is influencing consumer choices. Implement sustainable practices in your restaurant, such as reducing single-use plastics, sourcing locally, and minimizing food waste. Communicate your commitment to sustainability in your marketing efforts.
- **Personalization:** Consumers increasingly seek personalized experiences. Leverage customer data to understand preferences and offer tailored

recommendations. Implement loyalty programs that provide personalized rewards and incentives based on individual behavior.
- **Delivery and Takeout Options:** The rise of on-the-go lifestyles has fueled the demand for convenient dining options. Enhance your delivery and takeout services, optimizing packaging for freshness and convenience. Consider partnerships with third-party delivery services.
- **Cultural Sensitivity:** In a diverse and interconnected world, cultural sensitivity is crucial. Consider dietary preferences, cultural influences, and global culinary trends when designing your menu. Showcasing inclusivity and cultural awareness can broaden your customer base.
- **Engagement on Social Media:** Social media platforms play a significant role in shaping consumer opinions and choices. Maintain an active presence on platforms such as Instagram, Facebook, and Twitter. Engage with your audience, share visually appealing content, and listen to customer feedback.
- **Agility in Marketing:** Stay agile in your marketing strategies to respond quickly to trends and shifts in consumer behavior. Monitor industry developments, conduct regular market research, and be willing to adjust your marketing approach based on emerging preferences.

Adapting to changing consumer behaviors requires a proactive and forward-thinking approach. By staying attuned to market trends and embracing innovation, you position your restaurant to meet the evolving expectations of your audience and remain a relevant culinary destination.

Chapter 14: Nourishing Success: The Impact of Employee Meals on Restaurant Culture

In the intricate world of restaurant management, the concept of feeding employees extends far beyond a simple provision of sustenance. This chapter explores the transformative benefits of providing free family meals or deeply discounted menu options for restaurant staff. From fostering a sense of community to enhancing employee well-being and performance, the practice of nourishing employees reflects not only a commitment to their physical needs but also a strategic investment in the overall success of the restaurant.

The Ritual of Family Meals: Building Community and Camaraderie
Breaking Bread Together: The Cultural Significance of Family Meals

The tradition of family meals, where restaurant staff gathers to share a communal meal before or after service, holds profound cultural significance within the industry. This practice transcends the utilitarian act of eating and becomes a cornerstone for building community and camaraderie among team members.

Fostering Team Unity:

Family meals create a shared experience that transcends hierarchical roles. Whether dishwasher or chef, everyone comes together as equals, fostering a sense of unity and teamwork. This shared ritual reinforces the idea that each member, regardless of their position, plays an integral role in the success of the restaurant.

Breaking Down Hierarchies:

In the communal space of a family meal, hierarchies dissipate. The executive chef sits beside the line cook, and the dishwasher shares a table with the server. This egalitarian setting promotes open communication, erasing the barriers that may exist during the intensity of service hours.

Enhancing Communication:

Informal conversations during family meals provide an avenue for non-work-related discussions. This casual setting encourages team members to bond over shared interests, fostering a deeper understanding and appreciation for each other beyond their professional roles.

Cultivating Trust:

Breaking bread together builds trust. In a relaxed environment, employees are more likely to share their thoughts, concerns, and ideas. This trust extends beyond the dining table, contributing to a more open and collaborative workplace culture.

The Financial Impact: Deeply Discounted Menus and Employee Wellness
Affordable Access to Quality Food: Enhancing Employee Well-Being

In addition to the communal aspect of family meals, providing deeply discounted menu options or free meals to employees carries tangible benefits for their well-being. The financial impact of this practice extends beyond mere cost considerations and contributes to a healthier, more engaged workforce.

Health and Well-Being:

Access to nutritious and satisfying meals positively impacts the physical well-being of employees. By ensuring that the staff is well-fed, restaurant owners invest in their health, energy levels, and overall job satisfaction. This, in turn, can contribute to decreased absenteeism and improved performance.

Financial Relief for Employees:

The restaurant industry often operates on tight profit margins, and many employees may face financial constraints. Offering deeply discounted or free meals provides a financial benefit, effectively putting money back into the pockets of staff. This gesture demonstrates a commitment to the holistic well-being of employees beyond their roles in the restaurant.

Improved Job Satisfaction:

When employees feel valued through benefits like discounted or free meals, job satisfaction increases. A satisfied workforce is more likely to be committed, engaged, and willing to go the extra mile, contributing to a positive and productive work environment.

Retention and Recruitment:

The provision of affordable and nutritious meals can be a powerful tool for both employee retention and recruitment. In an industry with high turnover rates, offering tangible benefits like discounted or free meals can set a restaurant apart as an employer of choice.

Inclusivity: Dishwashers and Kitchen Staff Eating Free
A Culinary Family: Recognizing the Backbone of the Kitchen

In many establishments, the tradition of providing free meals extends specifically to certain roles, with dishwashers and kitchen staff often enjoying the privilege of eating for free. This practice recognizes the vital contributions of these individuals, often the unsung heroes who form the backbone of the kitchen.

Dishwashers:
Dishwashers play a pivotal role in maintaining the flow of service by ensuring that dishes are cleaned and ready for use. Despite their behind-the-scenes role, they are integral to the functioning of the restaurant. Offering them free meals is a gesture of acknowledgment for their hard work and dedication.

Kitchen Staff:
From line cooks to sous chefs, kitchen staff are the artisans who craft the culinary creations that define the restaurant. Recognizing their contribution by providing complimentary meals is not just a perk but a symbol of appreciation for the creativity, skill, and hard work they bring to the kitchen.

Creating a Culinary Community:
Extending free meals to dishwashers and kitchen staff reinforces the idea of a culinary community where every role is valued. It communicates that regardless of where an individual fits into the hierarchy, their contributions are integral to the collective success of the restaurant.

Boosting Morale and Motivation:
For dishwashers and kitchen staff, free meals serve as a morale booster. It not only provides a practical benefit but also communicates that their efforts are seen, valued, and reciprocated. This recognition can contribute to increased motivation and a positive work atmosphere.

Building a Sustainable Culture: From Tradition to Strategic Investment
Strategic Implications: Nurturing a Culture of Care and Excellence

Beyond the immediate benefits, the practice of providing free family meals or deeply discounted menu options carries strategic implications for the long-term success and sustainability of a restaurant. This practice goes beyond a mere cost and becomes an investment in the culture, performance, and reputation of the establishment.

Cultural Impact:
The tradition of feeding employees is a cultural investment. It shapes the identity of the restaurant, creating a narrative of care, inclusivity, and appreciation. This culture permeates every aspect of the establishment, contributing to a positive workplace atmosphere.

Employee Retention:

A restaurant with a strong culture of employee care is more likely to retain its staff. Employee retention is not just a cost-saving measure but also a strategic advantage. Experienced and loyal staff contribute to operational efficiency and enhance the overall guest experience.

Positive Public Image:
The reputation of a restaurant extends beyond its culinary offerings. A commitment to employee well-being, visible through practices like providing free or discounted meals, contributes to a positive public image. Customers are increasingly drawn to establishments that demonstrate ethical and employee-friendly practices.

Recruitment Magnet:
In a competitive labor market, attracting top talent is a continuous challenge. Restaurants known for their employee-centric practices, including affordable and nutritious meals, become magnets for skilled and dedicated professionals.

Workplace Excellence:
A well-fed and satisfied workforce is more likely to deliver excellence in their roles. From the kitchen to the front of the house, employees who feel cared for are motivated to uphold high standards, contributing to the overall success of the restaurant.

Case Studies: Stories of Success Through Employee Nourishment
Real-World Impact: How Employee Meals Transform Restaurants

Explore two hypothetical case studies illustrating the transformative impact of employee nourishment on restaurant culture.

Case Study 1: Unity Through Family Meals
In Restaurant X, the tradition of family meals is deeply ingrained in the culture. Staff members, regardless of their roles, gather for a communal meal before each service. This ritual has created a sense of unity, open communication, and a supportive atmosphere.

Outcome:

- **Improved Team Dynamics:** The sense of unity cultivated through family meals translates to improved team dynamics during service.
- **Enhanced Communication:** Open and informal conversations during family meals have led to improved communication among team members.
- **Cohesive Culture:** The family meal tradition has become a cornerstone of the restaurant's culture, fostering a sense of belonging and shared purpose.

Case Study 2: Employee Wellness Through Affordable Meals
Restaurant Y takes a strategic approach to employee wellness by offering deeply discounted menu options for staff. This practice has tangible benefits for the well-being, job satisfaction, and overall performance of the employees.

Outcome:

- **Healthier Workforce:** Access to nutritious and affordable meals has contributed to a healthier and more energized workforce.
- **Increased Job Satisfaction:** Employees express higher job satisfaction, feeling valued and cared for through the provision of discounted meals.
- **Positive Workplace Environment:** The practice of affordable meals has become a symbol of the restaurant's commitment to employee well-being, creating a positive and supportive work environment.

Overcoming Challenges: Sustaining Employee Meal Programs
Navigating Potential Hurdles: Strategies for Success

While the benefits of providing employee meals are evident, sustaining such programs may face challenges. Strategies for overcoming potential hurdles include:

Cost Management:
- **Menu Planning:** Strategically plan employee meals to balance nutritional value with cost-effectiveness.
- **Negotiating with Suppliers:** Negotiate with suppliers for cost-effective ingredients to minimize expenses.

Logistics:
- **Efficient Service:** Implement efficient service procedures to minimize disruptions during meal times.
- **Flexibility in Timing:** Provide flexibility in meal times to accommodate varying schedules.

Inclusivity:
- **Accommodating Dietary Restrictions:** Ensure that meals cater to diverse dietary preferences and restrictions.
- **Cultural Sensitivity:** Consider cultural preferences to create a menu that is inclusive and respectful of diverse backgrounds.

Communication:
- **Transparent Communication:** Clearly communicate the availability and details of employee meal programs.
- **Employee Feedback:** Seek feedback from employees to continuously refine and improve the meal offerings.

Scaling:
- **Scalability:** Design programs that are scalable as the restaurant grows, considering the potential increase in staff numbers.
- **Technology Integration:** Explore technology solutions to streamline processes, such as ordering systems or meal tracking.

Conclusion: A Recipe for Success Through Employee Nourishment
Beyond the Plate: Nurturing a Thriving Restaurant Ecosystem

In the intricate dance of restaurant management, the provision of free family meals or deeply discounted menu options emerges not just as a culinary tradition but as a powerful tool for shaping a thriving and sustainable restaurant ecosystem. From building a sense of community and fostering employee well-being to strategically positioning the restaurant as an employer of choice, the benefits extend far beyond the financial investment.

As restaurant owners navigate the dynamic landscape of the industry, the practice of feeding employees becomes a recipe for success—one that goes beyond the plate and touches the very core of the restaurant's identity. It is a commitment to creating not just a place to work but a culinary home where every member of the team is nourished, valued, and empowered to contribute to the collective success of the establishment. Through this simple yet profound act, restaurant owners craft a narrative of care, excellence, and inclusivity—a narrative that resonates not only within the walls of the kitchen but with every satisfied guest who walks through the door.

Chapter 15: Unlocking Performance: The Strategic Role of Bonuses in Motivating Management Teams

In the intricate tapestry of restaurant management, the concept of bonuses stands out as a powerful tool for motivating and incentivizing leadership. This chapter delves into the strategic considerations of offering bonuses to management staff, emphasizing the critical role that clear metrics and time frames play in sustaining motivation and driving performance. From aligning incentives with organizational goals to fostering a culture of accountability, well-structured bonus programs can become a catalyst for success in the dynamic and competitive restaurant industry.

Aligning Incentives with Organizational Goals

Beyond Compensation: Bonuses as Strategic Motivators

Bonuses for management staff extend beyond traditional compensation structures. When strategically designed, they serve as potent motivators, aligning the goals of individual managers with the overarching objectives of the restaurant. This alignment is crucial for cultivating a shared sense of purpose and driving collective success.

Performance-Driven Incentives:

Bonuses, when tied to specific performance metrics, become powerful tools for driving results. Rather than a mere financial reward, they become a tangible acknowledgment of achievements and contributions.

Organizational Objectives:

The most effective bonus programs are those intricately woven into the fabric of the restaurant's strategic objectives. Whether it's achieving financial targets, enhancing customer satisfaction, or improving operational efficiency, bonuses should directly support the restaurant's overarching goals.

Retention and Motivation:

Beyond the immediate financial gain, bonuses contribute to the retention and motivation of top-tier talent. Management teams that see a direct correlation between their efforts and financial rewards are more likely to remain engaged and committed to their roles.

Cultivating a Performance Culture:
Well-structured bonus programs contribute to the cultivation of a performance-driven culture within the management team. As managers strive to meet and exceed targets, they contribute to a positive and dynamic work environment.

The Importance of Clear Metrics: Navigating the Path to Success
Metric Precision: A Blueprint for Success in Bonus Programs

The success of a management bonus program hinges on the clarity and precision of the metrics used to evaluate performance. Vague or ambiguous criteria can lead to confusion, frustration, and a loss of motivation. Clearly defined metrics serve as a blueprint, providing a roadmap for managers to navigate towards success.

Quantifiable Targets:
Metrics should be quantifiable and directly tied to specific outcomes. Whether it's achieving revenue milestones, reducing operational costs, or improving customer satisfaction scores, the targets should be measurable and transparent.

Time-Bound Goals:
Setting clear time frames for achieving goals is equally crucial. Whether bonuses are tied to monthly, quarterly, or annual performance, a time-bound structure adds a sense of urgency and direction to the management team's efforts.

Alignment with Job Roles:
Metrics must align with the specific responsibilities and impact areas of each management role. For example, a front-of-house manager may have metrics related to customer satisfaction and service speed, while a back-of-house manager may focus on kitchen efficiency and inventory management.

Regular Performance Reviews:
Regular performance reviews, aligned with the bonus time frames, provide opportunities for managers to receive feedback, course-correct if needed, and stay on track towards achieving their targets. The review process should be transparent and collaborative.

Flexibility and Adaptability:
In the dynamic restaurant industry, the ability to adapt and respond to changing circumstances is crucial. Bonus metrics should allow for flexibility to accommodate unforeseen challenges while maintaining a focus on the overall strategic goals.

Time Frames: Sustaining Momentum Through Goal-oriented Timelines
Temporal Dynamics: The Rhythm of Bonus Programs

The time frames associated with bonus programs are more than just administrative details—they are the rhythmic pulse that sustains momentum and keeps managers engaged. Setting the right time frames involves striking a balance between short-term wins and long-term strategic objectives.

Short-Term Rewards:
Short-term bonus time frames, such as monthly or quarterly, provide managers with tangible and frequent rewards. These short cycles create a sense of immediacy and allow for quick adjustments based on performance trends.

Long-Term Strategic Goals:
While short-term rewards are essential, a well-rounded bonus program should also incorporate long-term time frames. This ensures that managers remain focused on achieving strategic goals that contribute to the sustained success of the restaurant over time.

Annual Performance Reviews:
Annual bonus time frames align with broader organizational objectives and provide an opportunity for a comprehensive review of a manager's contributions throughout the year. This longer time frame is particularly effective for evaluating the impact of strategic initiatives and sustained performance.

Seasonal Considerations:
For some restaurants, particularly those in seasonal locations, bonus time frames may need to align with peak operational periods. This ensures that managers are incentivized and rewarded during periods of heightened business activity.

Balancing Consistency and Variety:
Balancing consistency and variety in bonus time frames prevents monotony and keeps managers engaged. Periodic adjustments to the time frames or introducing special incentives for specific initiatives add an element of excitement and adaptability to the program.

Motivation and Accountability: Fostering a Culture of Ownership
Cultivating Ownership: The Nexus of Motivation and Accountability

The success of management bonus programs is intricately tied to the cultivation of a culture where managers feel a deep sense of ownership for their roles and the success of the restaurant. Motivation and accountability form a symbiotic relationship within this culture.

Personal Investment in Success:
Managers who feel a personal investment in the success of the restaurant are more likely to be motivated by bonus programs. The alignment of personal and organizational goals creates a sense of shared destiny.

Recognition and Acknowledgment:

Bonuses serve not only as financial rewards but also as symbols of recognition and acknowledgment. When managers see their efforts translating into tangible rewards, it reinforces a sense of being valued and appreciated.

Goal Setting and Planning:
The process of setting goals and planning for their achievement becomes a collaborative effort between management and ownership. This collaboration fosters a sense of shared responsibility and commitment to success.

Individual and Team Performance:
While bonuses are often tied to individual performance, they should also consider the impact of managerial contributions on overall team success. This balance ensures that managers collaborate rather than compete, contributing to a harmonious and effective management team.

Continuous Improvement:
Incentivizing continuous improvement is a key aspect of a successful bonus program. Managers who are motivated to enhance their skills, adapt to changing circumstances, and contribute to the ongoing success of the restaurant become assets to the organization.

Challenges and Mitigations: Navigating the Complexities of Bonus Programs
Addressing Potential Hurdles: Strategies for Success

While the benefits of management bonus programs are evident, potential challenges may arise. Proactive strategies can help address these challenges and ensure the sustained success of the program.

Communication Gaps:
- **Transparent Communication:** Address communication gaps by ensuring that bonus metrics and time frames are communicated clearly. Regular updates and check-ins contribute to ongoing clarity.

Unrealistic Targets:
- **Realistic Goal Setting:** Mitigate the risk of setting unrealistic targets by conducting a thorough assessment of the restaurant's current state and future growth potential. Goals should be challenging but achievable.

Resistance to Change:
- **Change Management Strategies:** Introduce changes to bonus programs gradually, with clear communication about the reasons for the changes and the potential benefits for both managers and the restaurant.

Lack of Buy-In:
- **Involvement in Goal Setting:** Involve managers in the goal-setting process to ensure buy-in. When managers have a say in the metrics and targets, they are more likely to feel a sense of ownership.

Financial Constraints:
- **Flexible Structures:** Design bonus programs with flexibility to accommodate the financial constraints of the restaurant. This may involve adjusting bonus percentages, introducing tiered structures, or exploring alternative incentive models.

Case Studies: Success Stories Through Strategic Bonus Programs
Real-World Impact: How Bonus Programs Transform Management Performance

Explore two hypothetical case studies illustrating the transformative impact of well-designed bonus programs on management performance.

Case Study 1: Strategic Alignment for Growth

Restaurant A implements a bonus program focused on achieving specific growth targets, including increased revenue and expanded market share. Clear metrics tied to these goals, combined with quarterly time frames, create a sense of urgency and focus among the management team.

Outcome:
- **Achievement of Growth Targets:** The bonus program serves as a catalyst for achieving growth targets, contributing to the restaurant's expanded market presence.
- **Motivated and Aligned Management Team:** The management team, motivated by the financial rewards and a sense of achievement, becomes a cohesive force aligned with the restaurant's strategic growth objectives.

Case Study 2: Customer-Centric Excellence

Restaurant B adopts a bonus program centered around customer satisfaction metrics, including service speed, cleanliness, and positive online reviews. Short-term time frames and regular performance reviews ensure that managers remain focused on delivering an exceptional customer experience.

Outcome:
- **Enhanced Customer Satisfaction:** The bonus program results in a tangible improvement in customer satisfaction metrics, leading to increased repeat business and positive word-of-mouth.
- **Engaged and Customer-Focused Managers:** Managers, motivated by the direct correlation between customer satisfaction and financial rewards, become more attentive to customer needs and contribute to a positive dining experience.

Conclusion: Bonus Programs as Catalysts for Excellence
Crafting a Symphony of Success Through Strategic Incentives

In the symphony of restaurant management, bonus programs emerge as powerful instruments that can elevate performance, drive success, and cultivate a culture of excellence. When designed with precision, incorporating clear metrics and strategic time frames, bonus programs become more than financial incentives—they become catalysts for individual and collective achievement.

As restaurant owners navigate the complexities of management, the strategic deployment of bonus programs becomes a nuanced art. It is about aligning incentives with organizational goals, fostering a culture of accountability, and providing a pathway for managers to thrive. From short-term wins to long-term strategic objectives, well-structured bonus programs contribute to the vibrancy and success of the restaurant industry, ensuring that every member of the management team plays a crucial role in the symphony of success.

Chapter 16: Ikigai: Embracing Purpose and Passion in Hospitality

In the bustling world of hospitality, where every interaction is an opportunity to create magic, finding your ikigai can be like discovering the secret ingredient to your favorite recipe—the one that makes everything come alive with flavor and meaning.

Unpacking Ikigai

Ikigai, a Japanese concept often translated as "a reason for being," is about uncovering the sweet spot where your passions, talents, values, and contributions intersect. It's that feeling you get when you're doing something you love, something you're good at, something the world needs, and something you can be paid for, all rolled into one.

Imagine a Venn diagram with four circles: passion, vocation, mission, and profession. Ikigai is the magic that happens at the intersection of these circles, where purpose and fulfillment collide.

Passion

Passion is the heartbeat of ikigai—the driving force that fuels your soul and infuses every aspect of your work with energy and enthusiasm. In hospitality, passion takes many forms, from a love for creating culinary masterpieces to a passion for crafting unforgettable guest experiences.

Imagine a chef who wakes up before dawn, eager to experiment with new ingredients and techniques, or a hotelier who takes pride in every detail of their property, from the decor to the guest amenities. These individuals are driven by a deep-seated passion for their craft, and it's this passion that sets them apart and fuels their success.

But passion alone is not enough. To truly unlock the power of ikigai, you must also have a deep understanding of your strengths and abilities.

Vocation

Your vocation is your superpower—the unique set of skills, talents, and strengths that set you apart from the crowd and enable you to excel in your chosen field. In hospitality, this might mean having a knack for problem-solving, a talent for storytelling, or an innate ability to connect with people from all walks of life.

Imagine a concierge who can anticipate a guest's needs before they even ask, or a bartender who can craft the perfect cocktail to match their mood. These individuals have honed their talents over time, refining their skills and abilities until they've become second nature.

But talent alone is not enough. To truly unlock the power of ikigai, you must also have a deep understanding of your values and beliefs.

Mission

Your mission is your North Star—the guiding principle that shapes your work and drives you to make a difference in the world. In hospitality, this might mean creating spaces where people feel welcome and valued, championing sustainability and environmental stewardship, or celebrating diversity and cultural exchange.

Imagine a hotel that partners with local charities to give back to the community, or a restaurant that sources its ingredients from local farmers and producers. These establishments have a clear sense of purpose and mission, and it's this sense of purpose that inspires both guests and employees alike.

But purpose alone is not enough. To truly unlock the power of ikigai, you must also have a deep understanding of your financial needs and obligations.

Profession

Your profession is your livelihood—the practical side of ikigai that ensures you can sustain yourself financially while pursuing your passions. In hospitality, this might mean working in hotels, restaurants, or event venues, or starting your own hospitality business or consultancy.

Imagine a chef who turns their passion for food into a successful career, or an event planner who turns their love for celebrations into a thriving business. These individuals have found a way to monetize their talents and passions, allowing them to pursue their dreams while supporting themselves financially.

But financial stability alone is not enough. To truly unlock the power of ikigai, you must find a way to balance all four elements—passion, vocation, mission, and profession—in your work and life.

Embracing Ikigai in Everyday Life

Finding your ikigai is not just a one-time event—it's an ongoing journey of self-discovery, exploration, and growth. Here are some practical ways to embrace ikigai in your everyday life within the hospitality industry:

Embrace Your Passions: Take time to nurture your passions and pursue activities that bring you joy and fulfillment. Whether it's exploring new cuisines, learning a new language, or volunteering in your community, find ways to incorporate your passions into your daily life.

Celebrate Your Strengths

Recognize and celebrate your strengths, talents, and abilities, and find ways to leverage them in your work. Whether it's your gift for making people feel welcome, your talent for problem-solving, or your knack for creativity, embrace what makes you unique and use it to make a positive impact in the world.

Live Your Values

Align your work with your values and beliefs, and seek out opportunities that allow you to make a meaningful difference in the world. Whether it's supporting sustainable practices, promoting diversity and inclusion, or advocating for social justice, find ways to live your values in your daily life and work.

Set Meaningful Goals

Set goals that align with your ikigai and reflect your passion, purpose, and values within the hospitality industry. Whether it's mastering a new skill, launching a new initiative, or making a positive impact in your community, set goals that inspire and motivate you to achieve your dreams.

Practice Gratitude
Cultivate a sense of gratitude for the opportunities, experiences, and relationships in your life, and take time to express appreciation for the people who have supported you along the way. Whether it's thanking a colleague for their help, expressing gratitude to a guest for their kindness, or simply taking a moment to appreciate the beauty of the world around you, practice gratitude as a way of nurturing your sense of connection and fulfillment.

Conclusion

In conclusion, ikigai offers a powerful framework for finding purpose, passion, and fulfillment in the hospitality industry by aligning your passions, talents, values, and contributions with the needs of guests and the world at large. By embracing ikigai in your everyday life, you can cultivate a deeper sense of meaning and satisfaction in your work, ultimately leading to greater success and happiness in the dynamic and rewarding world of hospitality.

Whether you're a seasoned hospitality professional or just starting out on your journey, I encourage you to explore the concept of ikigai and reflect on how it can inform and enrich your work within the industry. By finding your ikigai and living it every day, you can create a life filled with purpose, passion, and joy.

www.ingramcontent.com/pod-product-compliance
Lightning Source LLC
Chambersburg PA
CBHW050246230526
45470CB00005B/2137